Celebrate Winter

All About Animals in Winter

by Martha E. H. Rustad

...ntree
...company — publishers for children

Raintree is an imprint of Capstone Global Library Limited, a company incorporated in England and Wales having its registered office at 7 Pilgrim Street, London, EC4V 6LB – Registered company number: 6695582

www.raintree.co.uk
myorders@raintree.co.uk

Text © Capstone Global Library Limited 2016
The moral rights of the proprietor have been asserted.

Editorial Credits
Erika L. Shores, editor; Cynthia Della-Rovere, designer;
Tracy Cummins, media researcher; Tori Abraham, production specialist

ISBN 978 1 4747 0309 3 (hardback)
19 18 17 16 15
10 9 8 7 6 5 4 3 2 1

ISBN 978 1 4747 0314 7 (paperback)
20 19 18 17 16 15
10 9 8 7 6 5 4 3 2 1

British Library Cataloguing in Publication Data
A full catalogue record for this book is available from the British Library.

Photo Credits
Dreamstime: Robin Van Olderen, 12, SandraRBarba, 6—7, Smellme, 16 (right); Newscom: ZUMA Press/Tony Crocetta, 26—27; Shutterstock: Aaron Amat, 27 (top), ala737, 13 (bottom), Alta Oosthuizen, 15 (top), 18, Ana Gram, 25, 29 (inset), bjogroet, 11 (top), Black Sheep Media (grass), throughout, Chantal de Bruijne (African landscape), back cover and throughout, creative, 10, e2dan, 13 (top), Eric Isselee, cover, back cover, 1, 4, 7 (top), 11 (bottom), 21 (top), 23 (top), 32, Gerrit_de_Vries, 14 (top), 17, Jez Bennett, 14 (bottom), John Michael Evan Potter, 9, Maggy Meyer, 28—29, MattiaATH, 8, Mogens Trolle, 15 (bottom), moizhusein, 20—21, 23, Moments by Mullineux, 5, Sean Stanton, 19, Serge Vero, 24, Stuart G. Porter, 22

Printed and bound in China.

Contents

Finding food

What do animals do in winter?

Birds visit a bird table.

They eat seeds.

Feathers puff up to stay warm.

An owl hunts mice.

It swallows them whole.

A deer scrapes bark.

It eats at dusk and dawn.

A fluffy fox hunts rabbits.

A squirrel stays in its nest.
It eats food it has stored.

Winter rest

Bats sleep in caves.

They rest all winter.

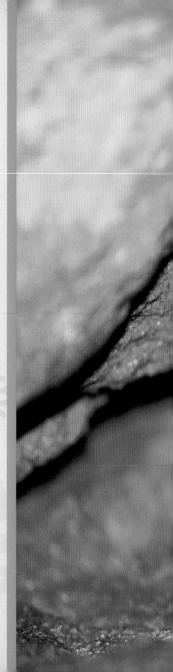

A frog sleeps
underground.
A frog wakes in spring.

Bears sleep in dens.

A bear's heart beats slowly.

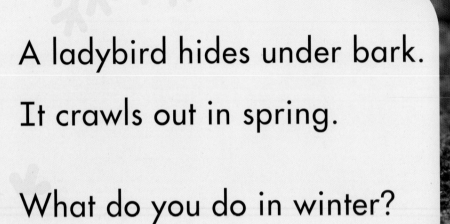

A ladybird hides under bark.

It crawls out in spring.

What do you do in winter?

Glossary

bark outer layer of a tree trunk

bird table table or other structure that holds food for birds; people put bird seed onto bird tables to feed birds in winter

den animal home

seed tiny plant part from which new plants grow

spring one of the four seasons of the year; spring is after winter and before summer

winter one of the four seasons of the year; winter is after autumn and before spring

Read more

Life Story of a Frog (Animal Life Stories), Charlotte Guillain (Raintree, 2014)

What Can Live in the Snow? (What Can Live There?), John-Paul Wilkins (Raintree, 2014)

Websites

www.naturedetectives.org.uk/winter/
Download winter wildlife ID sheets, pick up some great snowy-weather-game ideas and discover all the fun you can have with winter sticks!

www.wildlifewatch.org.uk/
Explore the Wildlife Trust's wildlife watch website and get busy this winter spotting interesting winter plants and animals living near by! Follow badger's blog for great wildlife spotting tips and some fascinating photographs.

Index